Version 1.0 - published October 2025

To read this document online, or to check that you are reading the most up-to-date version, visit:
www.themindfulnessinitiative.org

Copyright @ 2025 The Mindfulness Initiative
London, United Kingdom
The Mindfulness Initiative is a Charitable Incorporated Organisation, registered number: 1179834 (England & Wales)

Written by Vin Harris and Richard Edwards
Edited by Menka Sanghvi
Design by J-P Stanway

ISBN 978-1-913353-08-7

 This work is licensed under a Creative Commons Attribution-Non Commercial-NoDerivatives 4.0 International License.

Acknowledgements:

We are grateful to Menka Sanghvi, who leads on innovation for the Mindfulness Initiative and is the author of the *Fieldbook for Mindfulness Innovators*. Her work inspired - and continues to support - the development of the Innovations Awards programme and the production of this workbook.

We would also like to thank the participants of the online *Sharing Your Treasure* pilot course for helping to shape this resource and for allowing us to include some of their voices in this workbook, so that they may walk alongside you in these pages.

About the Authors

Vin Harris

Having practiced and studied meditation for over 50 years, and with a strong background in business, Vin has been a teaching fellow at the University of Aberdeen and has taught and developed mindfulness training in the UK and across Europe. In 2013, Vin co-founded the Hart Knowe Trust with the aim of "helping people so that they can help others". Inspired by the *Fieldbook for Mindfulness Innovators*, Vin worked to bring its principles to life through the *Innovations in Mindfulness Awards*, a collaboration with the Mindfulness Initiative. These Awards not only celebrate outstanding projects but also offer a framework for responsible, inclusive, and needs-driven innovation.

Richard Edwards

Director of the Mindfulness Initiative between 2023 and 2025, and a Fellow of the Royal Society for Arts, Richard is an accredited Breathworks Mindfulness Teacher and registered Change Management Practitioner. Richard has extensive leadership and management experience and has brought mindfulness to a range of audiences including those in leadership roles and individuals who are living with complex and compound trauma.

About The Mindfulness Initiative

The Mindfulness Initiative (MI) began as a programme of mindfulness teaching for politicians in the UK Parliament. Since then, it has grown into a charity with a mission to weave mindfulness into public and social policy, nurture innovation, and advocate for best practice in mindfulness-based approaches.

Our vision is of a thriving, interconnected world in which awareness, compassion, and openness shape both our daily lives and our shared future.

We believe that for mindfulness to remain sustainable and accessible, it must be able to respond to today's world, not simply repeat what worked in the past. In 2019, the *Fieldbook for Mindfulness Innovators* was published as a practical guide for those seeking to bring mindfulness into new contexts and communities while protecting its integrity. The Fieldbook was updated in 2024. Its central message remains simple but powerful: innovation is not about disruption for its own sake, but is essential for relevance, reach, and resonance.

Following two rounds of Awards in 2022 and 2024, which highlighted a wide range of inspiring initiatives, we asked ourselves: What more could we do to support the next wave of innovators, those just beginning their journey, or those at a crossroads?

This workbook is part of our answer.

Getting in touch

If you have any questions, suggestions or other feedback on this document, please get in touch by emailing info@mindfulnessinitiative.org.uk.

Welcome

Welcome to *Sharing Your Treasure: A Workbook for Mindfulness Innovators*. This book is created with you in mind, the mindfulness teacher who feels a deep wish to share the benefits of practice, yet sometimes wonders how to do so in ways that connect with people's lives today.

The landscape of mindfulness teaching has shifted. Traditional eight-week courses no longer draw the numbers they once did. Many people still feel that mindfulness "isn't for them." And yet, each year, new teachers step forward, inspired by the treasure they have discovered through their own practice, longing to pass it on.

There's a well-known saying: "The definition of insanity is doing the same thing over and over again and expecting a different result." But here's something else to consider – what if doing the same thing and expecting the same result isn't very smart either? Spencer Johnson's 1998 book about change and adaptability, *Who Moved My Cheese?* looks at how we resist or adapt to change. Seeing the cheese as the goal highlights the problem of repeatedly following the same path, even when the cheese is no longer at the end of it.

It can be unsettling when familiar ways of teaching no longer seem to work. Perhaps in this case, the cushion has moved. But as mindfulness reminds us, turning toward discomfort often reveals new insights. The question "Who moved my cushion?" is not a lament but an invitation to look freshly at what is happening, to listen more deeply to those we wish to serve, and to imagine new ways of sharing mindfulness with creativity and integrity.

This workbook is a companion, not a set of instructions. It offers a space to pause, reflect, and experiment. At its heart is the Innovation Mandala, a reflective framework designed to help you uncover your own treasure – the unique gifts, experiences, and perspectives you have to offer. The Mandala does not ask you to fit into someone else's mould. Instead of focusing on "What do I want to get?" it asks, "What do I have to give?" The Mandala contains multiple zones and fields, and is intended as a holistic framework.

This workbook will support you in understanding yourself better as a mindfulness teacher with a unique contribution to offer, alongside which the Fieldbook for Mindfulness Innovators offers practical guidance for responsible and sustainable innovation. Together, they can support you to shape ideas that are effective, inclusive, and true to your values.

The pages ahead include reflections, practical exercises for your Innovation Journal, and stories from others who have walked this path. They are here to encourage you to notice what feels alive, to trust your own experience, and to take small steps that may grow into something larger.

Our hope is that *Sharing Your Treasure* will feel like a community in book form, a reminder that you are not alone. May it help you rediscover the spark that first drew you to mindfulness, and find fresh, joyful, and sustainable ways to share the treasure you carry for the benefit of yourself, your communities, and the wider world.

Vin Harris, Hart Knowe Trust, and
Richard Edwards, Mindfulness Initiative

❝ **We know the challenges that so many people are facing – whether it's mental health struggles, workplace stress, or the rising anxiety around the climate crisis. How do we stay hopeful? And what does hope look like? These feel like fundamental questions of our time as we all learn to deal with increased uncertainty in the world. What gives me hope is that even in the midst of these challenges, we have the ability to create small pockets of peace and clarity through simple practices.**

Ruth Davey, Look Again, Innovation in Mindfulness Awards winner, 2024.

Contents

Introduction	**06**
1. What Brings You Here?	**08**
2. Sharing Your Treasure	**14**
3. Connecting with Your Audience	**22**
4. Altruistic Action	**32**
5. Plan & Review	**40**
Taking Stock of Your Journey	**48**
What's Next?	**48**

Introduction

How to Use This Workbook

This workbook involves a lot of reflection, and we have allowed space in this book for you to make notes as you go along. We invite you to use the spaces provided to bring together your ideas and thoughts. There is no one right answer, this is an opportunity for you to consider what rings true for you right now, as you work through this book. You could use a separate dedicated physical notebook or an electronic notebook instead if you prefer. At the end of the process, you should have created a written record of the intention and initial ideas with which you are embarking on your Innovation journey.

You can work through this material individually, or you may prefer to work with a group by joining a course. Either way, this journey is personal to you, and you do not need to work through each stage of the Innovation Mandala in a linear way.

> **Now, I feel excited, energised and clear about who I want to serve – and the treasure I have to share.**
>
> Jan Haworth, *Sharing Your Treasure course participant*

> **Something which was feeling just too overwhelming at the beginning of this programme now feels not just exciting again but doable.**
>
> Sally Roberts, *Sharing Your Treasure course participant*

> **Through five weeks of gatherings, there have been many transformative moments. I've been able to flip my previous 'start-up founder' script, reframe some unhelpful ideas about myself, and adopt some more optimistic perspectives.**
>
> Kev Reader, *Sharing Your Treasure course participant*

The Mandala - An Overview

The Mandala is not a step-by-step process. It is more like a compass for reflection. It has three zones and twelve fields:

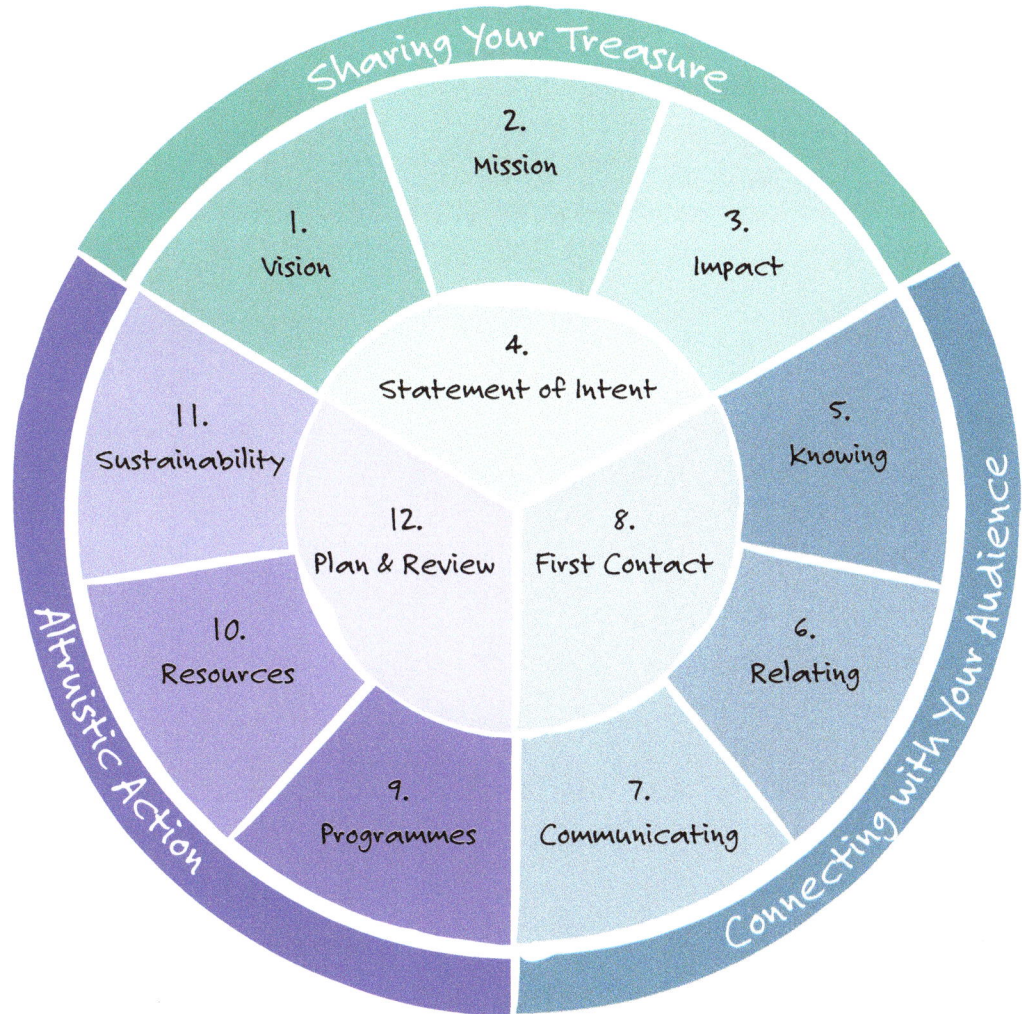

Zone One
Sharing Your Treasure

1. **Vision** – The treasure you have found and your vision for change

2. **Mission** – The specific issues you want to address

3. **Impact** – The difference you hope to make

4. **Statement of Intent** – Your inner compass aligning aspiration with action

Zone Two
Connecting with Your Audience

5. **Knowing** – Who you already know and can serve

6. **Relating** – How you present mindfulness so it resonates

7. **Communicating** – How you convey value and relevance

8. **First Contact** – How you introduce your work

Zone Three
Altruistic Action

9. **Programmes** – The offerings you design

10. **Resources** – Tangible and intangible supports, including your own wellbeing

11. **Sustainability** – Ensuring your work is financially and personally sustainable

12. **Plan & Review** – Testing, improving, and growing your work

Section 1

What Brings You Here?

> **Each of us has such a precious and unique identity. Each one of us, by virtue of our being, our practice, our work, and our love, is making a unique difference in the world. It may seem small, but it is not insignificant.**

Jon Kabat-Zinn

When we first step forward to teach mindfulness, it is tempting to think we need to become someone different: more professional, more polished, more like other teachers we admire. But the work begins with who you already are.

When you recognise that who you are and what you have to offer is already good enough, you no longer need to strive to fit a mould. You can begin from your own story, your own lived experience, and the treasure that has already touched your life.

This section helps you clarify your heartfelt motivation and the essence of the treasure you feel moved to share.

Reflection Exercise: Your Call to Adventure

Take a moment here to sit and reflect on:

- What first drew you to mindfulness?

- Can you recall a moment when you glimpsed freedom, compassion, or clarity, and thought to yourself that others should know this is possible too?

- What is the heart-essence of the treasure you have discovered?

Reflection

> ❝ I began this course not being sure how I fit – there are currently these different strands to my vocation, rather than just one. I've been reflecting since then, though, and I feel that the heart essence/treasure that I want to share with others is listening. So perhaps I could let go of unnecessary striving 'to fit' and simply lean into presence in listening and be.

Martha Pollard, *Sharing Your Treasure course participant*

An Inside-Out Approach to Innovation

Luke Doherty, from Mindful Peak Performance, winner of the Innovations in Mindfulness Awards in 2022, advised, *"Take notice of those moments when you get deeply moved to do something but don't have an immediate answer."*

Rather than rushing into strategies or marketing plans, innovation begins by asking "why" before "how." When we tend to our inner landscape, cultivating awareness, compassion, and connection, we find the deeper purpose that can anchor our work in authenticity.

You might find it helpful to look at the Fieldbook Section 2.1 on Theory U.

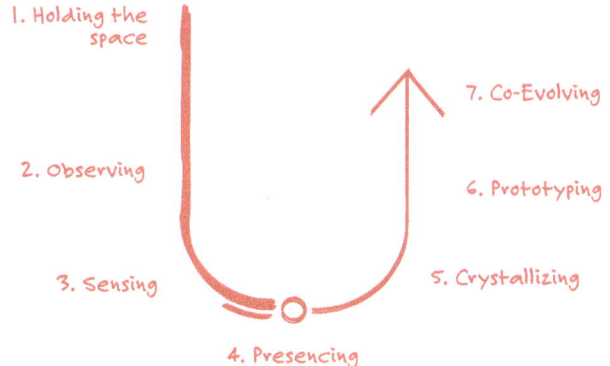

A Hero's Journey

In Joseph Campbell's work *The Hero with a Thousand Faces* (1949), Campbell introduces the idea of the monomyth, also known as the Hero's Journey, which portrays a common narrative in myths, legends, and stories across cultures. The pattern of the Hero's Journey is:

- **Departure** – feeling that something is wrong or a sense that there's more to life than this (Mindfulness)

- **Descent** – unfamiliar world where different rules apply, full of challenges, meeting guides and mentors (Compassion)

- **Initiation** – letting go of who you feel you are supposed to be, glimpses of inner freedom, spontaneous wish to share (Insight)

- **Return** – maintaining integrity and making what you have discovered accessible (Wisdom)

Your path as a mindfulness teacher may mirror this. Innovation isn't just about programmes, it's about the inner journey of remembering what called you here in the first place.

Reflection Exercise: Your Mindfulness Journey

- Take a moment here to sit and reflect on:

- What (really) brings you here?

- What do you feel you have to offer?

- How does your own journey mirror the stages of departure, descent, initiation, and return?

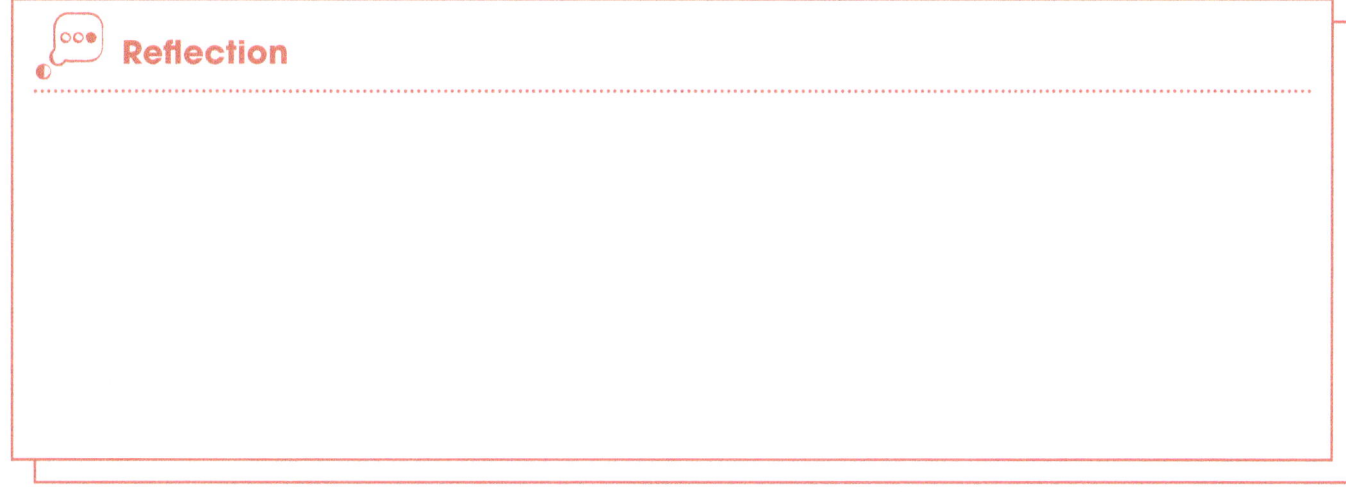

Journalling Activity

Look over your reflections in this section and articulate the treasure that you want to share. Feel free to use words, sketches, or anything that brings this alive for you. This forms the beginning of your Mindfulness Innovation Journal, which you will build on as you move through this workbook.

Section 2

Sharing Your Treasure

❝ **I loved science, and when I discovered Buddhist meditative practices and martial arts, I was able to bridge those ways of knowing the world into my own unique way. From that grew the Mindfulness-Based Stress Reduction (MBSR) program, which became my karmic assignment.**

Jon Kabat-Zinn

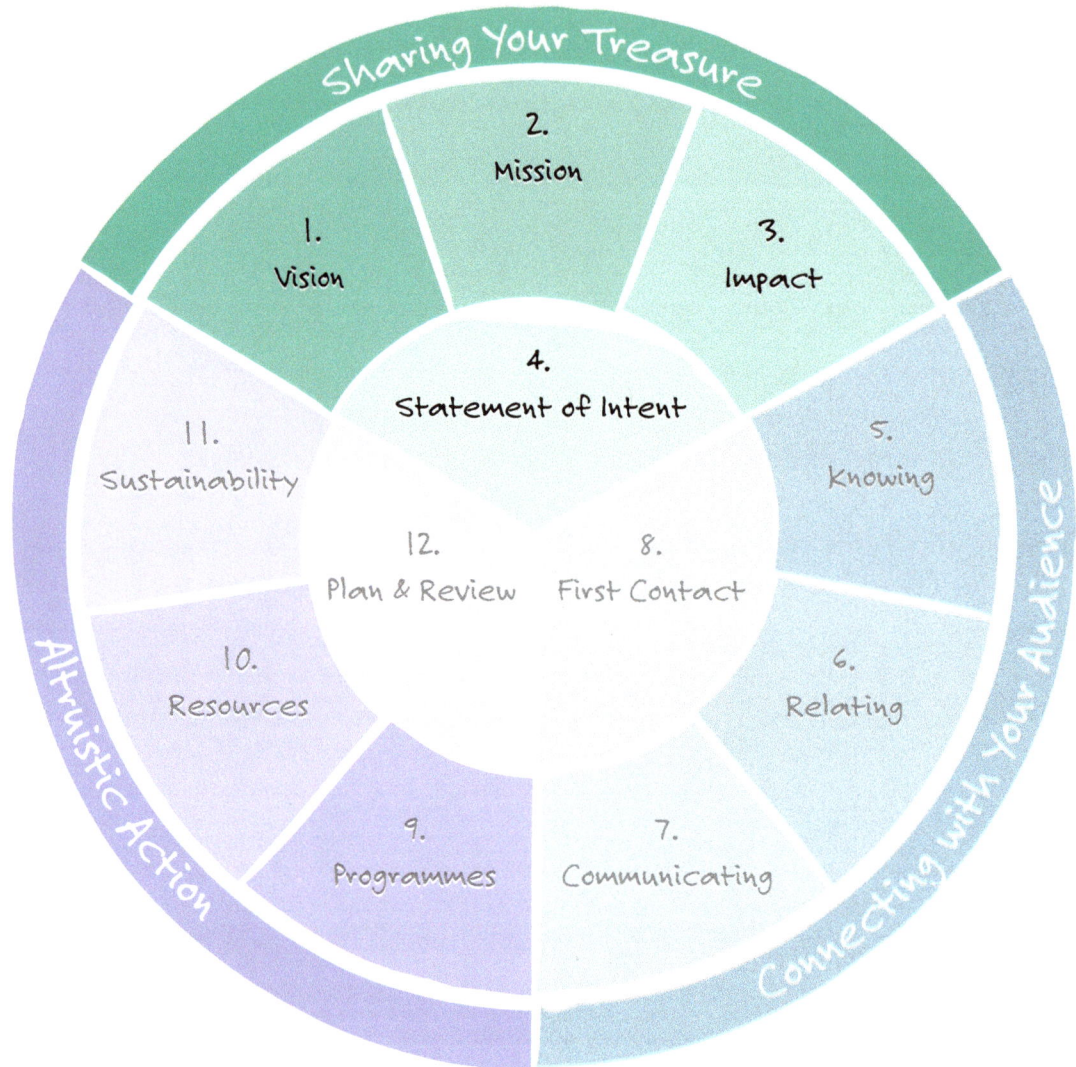

In this section, we develop your personal story toward a clearer sense of vision, mission, impact, and intent. This is about sharing your treasure and is expressed by Jon Kabat-Zinn as your 'karmic assignment' – the unique way you are positioned to be of service.

In the first section, we took an inside-out approach to innovation, and you will have explored what it is that has brought you to this point and the treasure that you wish to share.

Vision: Discovering Your Purpose

Your vision is the bigger picture: the positive change you hope to bring into the world by sharing mindfulness. It doesn't have to be complicated or lofty. A simple vision can act as a guiding light.

Mission: Defining Your Contribution

Your mission is more specific: the issues you want to address, the communities you wish to serve, and the contribution you feel uniquely able to make.

Impact: Taking Aligned Action

Impact is about what difference you want to make. What outcomes do you hope to see in the lives of those you teach? Think in terms of small, tangible steps rather than grand achievements.

Statement of Intent: Bringing It All Together

A statement of intent is your inner compass: a short declaration of who you are, what you do, and why you do it. It aligns your activity with your deepest aspirations.

This does not have to be complex and long. In fact, the simpler and shorter it is, the clearer the compass may be to read. An example of this is the NASA mission in the 1960s, defined by JFK as 'landing a man on the moon and returning him safely to earth'. This mission, this purpose, was held by everyone involved in the space program, from engineers to janitors.

Reflection Exercise: A Framework

A useful framework for approaching these fields can be to consider the following questions:

1. Who am I, and what brings me here?
2. What industry/field do I know?
3. What problems exist in my industry/field?
4. How am I uniquely positioned to be of service?
5. Who can I collaborate with?
6. How can I test my ideas?

Reflection

> 66 I intend to continue to advocate for those humans who have suffered at the hands of other humans in dominant positions of power and influence within the fields of mindfulness and healthcare and who have been ignored or dismissed. I will aim to highlight the unseen biases and blind spots that fail to acknowledge the incomplete evidence in providing a balanced perspective of both the benefits and risks in continued mindfulness practice and which therefore hinder the ethical development of robust safeguarding processes around mindfulness teaching, practice and research.

Christa Lawson, *Sharing Your Treasure course participant*

Circles of Concern and Influence

Steven Covey's Circles of Concern and Influence is a framework from his classic book The 7 Habits of Highly Effective People that helps people understand where to focus their energy and attention.

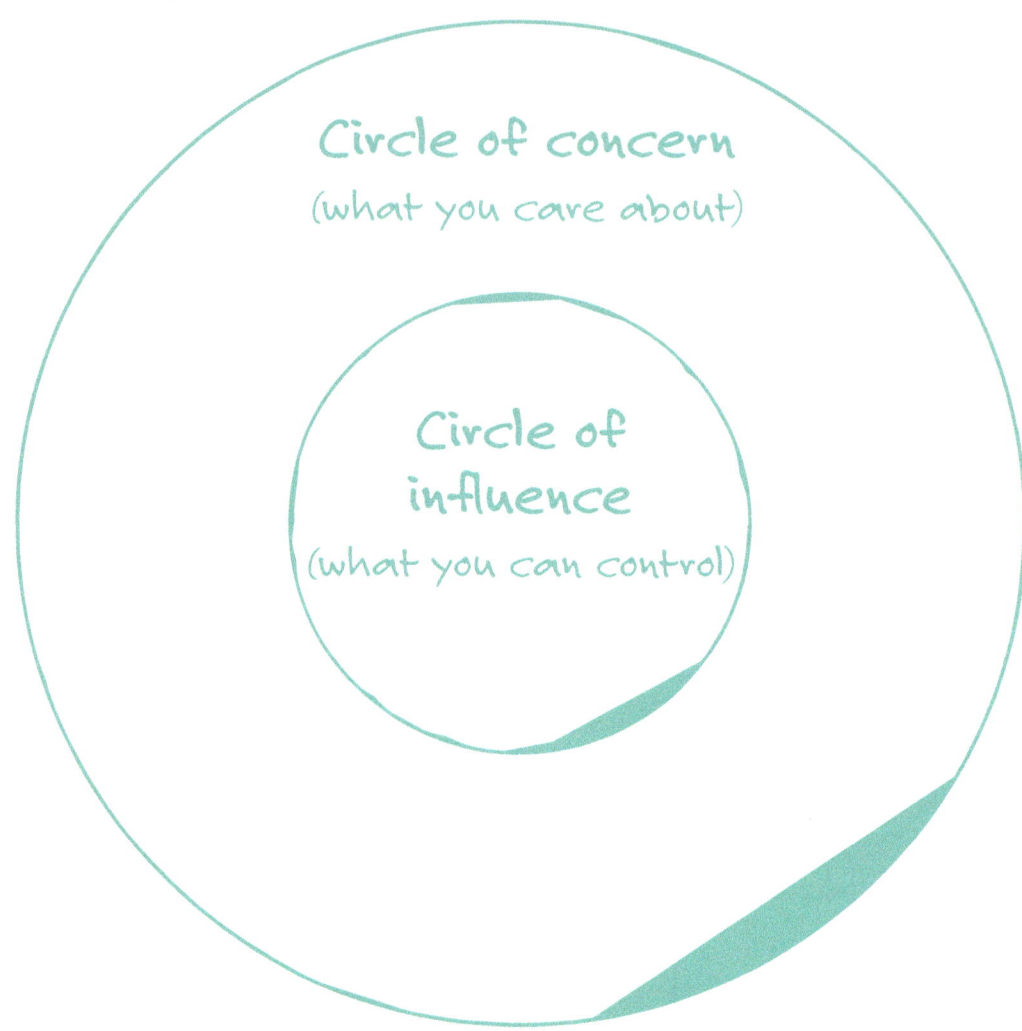

1. Circle of Concern

- Represents everything you care about or worry about – from global issues (wars, the economy, climate change) to personal matters (health, finances, relationships).

- It's broad and includes things you cannot directly control, such as government policies, other people's choices, or the weather.

- Often involves dwelling on the past or buying into a negative perspective of the future (negativity bias).

- If you spend most of your time here, you tend to feel anxious, reactive, and powerless, because you're focused on things outside your control.

2. Circle of Influence

- A smaller circle inside the Circle of Concern.

- It represents present choices open to you in the areas where you do have direct control or can effect change – your actions, habits, communication, problem-solving, and how you treat others.

- By acting responsibly and constructively in this circle, you can gradually expand your influence over time (for example, by improving your skills, strengthening relationships, or building trust).

- Focusing here makes you proactive and empowered because you concentrate on what you can do rather than what you can't.

Reflection Exercise: Concern and Influence

In relation to sharing your treasure, take a moment to sit and reflect on:

- What concerns weigh on your heart?

- Which of these lie within your circle of influence, and what difference do you notice when you shift your attention from your circle of concern to your circle of influence?

- What small step could you commit to today?

Reflection

Statement of Intent

Writing a statement of intent can represent a declaration of sharing your treasure, or, in Jon Kabat-Zinn's words, your Karmic Assignment. Here are some principles that might help you to bring this into focus:

- There are infinite needs to be addressed – you have to start somewhere, so begin with you (inside-out).

- Focus on compassion and what you care about.

- You are unique. What is your core competence? This can represent good business in a crowded marketplace.

- Often, core competence comes from multiple threads woven into a rich and unique tapestry. Synergy occurs when various disciplines converge. This can be unexpected.

As you explore the idea of competence, you may find it helpful to review the concept of 'warp and weft' on p18 of the Fieldbook.

Journalling Activity

There are two parts to this section's journalling, which you should write up here:

- Write a (provisional) Statement of Intent. Keep it simple, brief, memorable, inspiring.

- Make a commitment to take one small step based on Steven Covey's model of Concern and Influence. Don't be defined as the person who is one day (in the undefined future) going to achieve great things. Take a small step now. Start your journey.

Section 3

Connecting with Your Audience

❝ **If you do follow your bliss, you put yourself on a kind of track that has been there all the while waiting for you, and the life you ought to be living is the one you are living. When you can see that, you begin to meet people who are in the field of your bliss, and they open doors to you. I say follow your bliss and don't be afraid, and doors will open where you didn't know they were going to be.**

Joseph Campbell

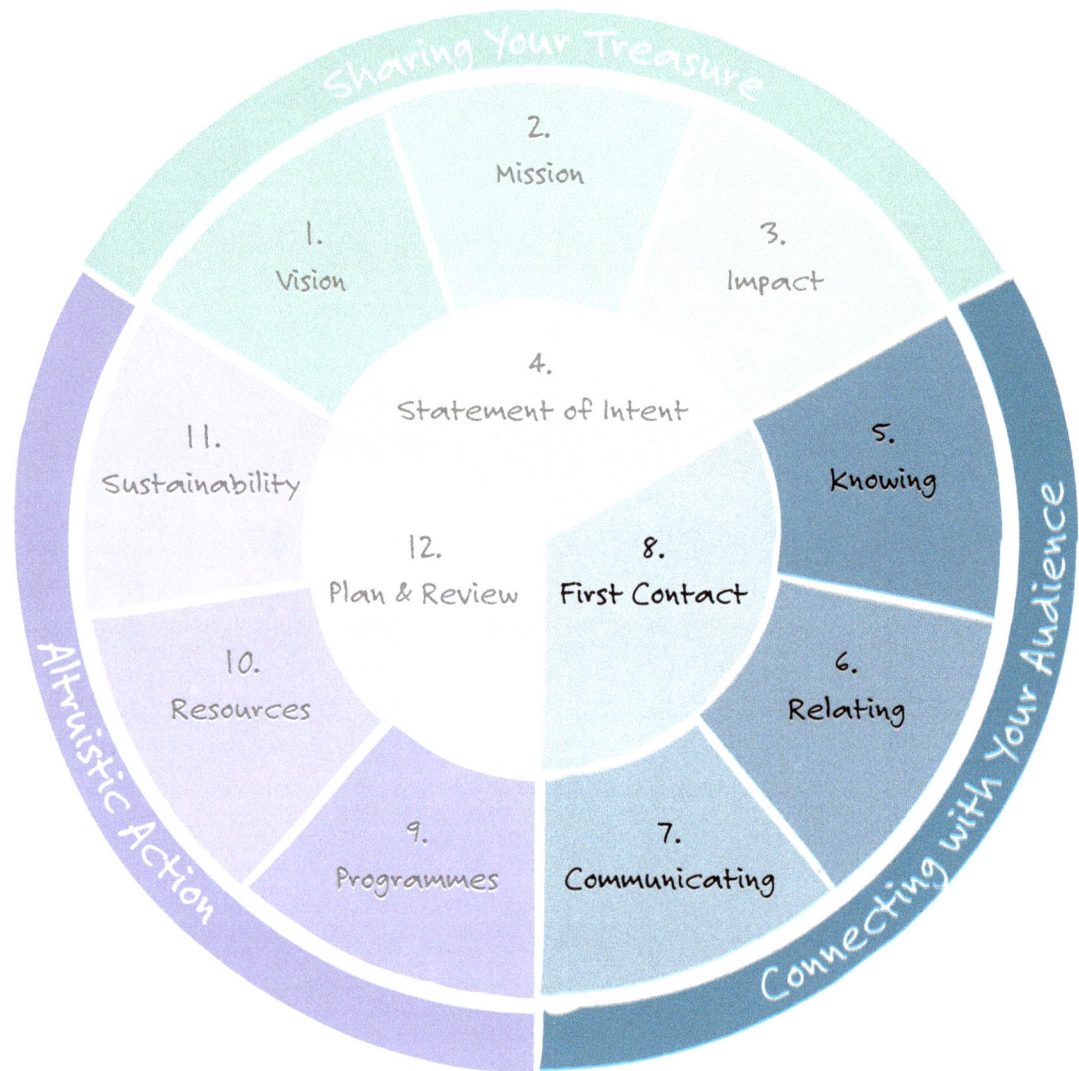

In this section, we will be looking at connecting with your audience through knowing, relating, communicating, and making first contact. By the end of this section, you will be able to produce a short presentation about your idea.

In the previous section, you identified the work you feel called to accomplish. The resources, reflections and discussions in this section will help you find your way to connect with the people you want to serve.

When starting a new venture, many people feel that they must tell the whole world about what they have to offer. This is almost never a good plan! There are already more than enough individuals and organisations spending a lot of time and money promoting themselves and their mindfulness trainings. As a qualified mindfulness teacher, you might ask yourself: How can I hope to compete with all these wonderful (and not so wonderful) teachings that are out there?

Since our purpose is not to add to the busyness and confusion of modern life, a better question would be: What is the easiest, most cost-effective way to connect with my intended audience? The answer is almost always: Know your audience well, present mindfulness so they understand why it is relevant and then find a direct way to communicate with them.

From Dependent to Independent and Interdependent

We have already met Steven Covey in this workbook, looking at his circles of concern and influence. This was part of being proactive, as the first of the 7 Habits of Highly Effective People. This model maps the journey from being dependent to interdependent. These 7 habits are:

1. **Be Proactive**: Take responsibility for your actions and focus on what you can control, rather than reacting to external circumstances.

2. **Begin with the End in Mind**: Define your vision, values, and long-term goals, then align daily actions with them.

3. **Put First Things First**: Prioritise important tasks (not just urgent ones) and manage time around what matters most.

4. **Think Win-Win**: Seek mutually beneficial solutions in relationships and negotiations.

5. **Seek First to Understand, Then to Be Understood**: Practice empathetic listening before expressing your own views.

6. **Synergise**: Value teamwork and diversity; combine strengths to achieve more together than alone.

7. **Sharpen the Saw**: Regularly renew yourself physically, mentally, emotionally, and spiritually to maintain effectiveness.

Here we shall focus on Habits 4 and 5. Gaining a deep understanding of your audience and their needs – knowing, relating and being able to communicate with them is fundamental to connecting with your audience.

Reflection Exercise: Your Audience

Take a moment now to sit and bring to mind your intended audience.

- Consider your audience's daily struggles, concerns, and aspirations (what they think and feel). What influences their beliefs about mindfulness (what they see and hear). How they currently engage in wellness (what they say and do), and what might prevent them from taking part in mindfulness (barriers).

- How could you ensure that your work resonates without compromising authenticity?

Fostering Inclusivity

Verna Myers, a well-known diversity and inclusion strategist and currently VP of Inclusion Strategy at Netflix, is often credited with creating a simple but powerful way of framing diversity, inclusion, and belonging. Her model highlights the distinction between these terms and why all three matter:

- Diversity is about representation – Who is in the room? It's the presence of people from different identities, backgrounds, perspectives, and experiences.

- Inclusion is about participation – Being asked to dance. It's ensuring those diverse voices are actively invited, respected, and valued. Myers is famous for the phrase:

"Diversity is being invited to the party; inclusion is being asked to dance."

- Belonging goes a step further – Dancing like nobody's watching. It's the emotional experience of feeling safe, accepted, and empowered to bring your authentic self, without fear of exclusion or tokenism. Perhaps another way of expressing this could be:

"Belonging is getting to choose the music."

Please read Section 3.4 of the Fieldbook: Awareness of Power Dynamics.

Reflection Exercise: Diversity, Inclusion and Belonging

Repeat the last reflection exercise, bringing to mind your intended audience.

- What does diversity, inclusion and belonging look and feel like to your intended audience, and what could you do to realise this in your work?

You may find this is hard, and of course, it is very hard to see what is not part of your own personal experience. Remember Habit 5. How can you seek to understand what inclusivity means to your audience?

Reflection

Using Your NOSE

Connecting with your audience is not something that you do to them. It is a process of alignment and collaboration, a process of synergy.

Tom Sant, in his book Persuasive Business Proposals, suggested that business proposals should lead with the audience's needs and outcomes before offering solutions, followed by evidence to support the claims. This is presented as the NOSE Model:

Needs
Start with them, not you

- Audiences connect when they feel seen and understood.
- Identify their challenges, motivations, or pain points first.
- Instead of beginning with your solution, show you understand their world.

(Please read Chapter 3 of the Fieldbook - Designing with and for People)

Outcomes
Paint the picture of success

- Clearly describe what they will gain if their needs are addressed.
- Outcomes should be framed in their language – what's meaningful to them (better focus, stress reduced, goals achieved). Do not overclaim the outcomes of your work.

Solutions
Offer the pathway

- Now present your idea, product, or message as the way to achieve those outcomes.
- Position it as a response to the needs they already agreed they have.

Evidence
Build trust

- People connect emotionally first, but they also need credibility.
- Use data, case studies, or testimonials to prove your solution works. Be careful not to misuse evidence from one mindfulness programme to assert the precise efficacy of something different.

(Please read Chapter 4 of the Fieldbook: Does it Work?)

Inner Transition

Innovation involves doing things differently; it involves change. When we think about planning – what we are going to do differently and how we will connect with our intended audience – it is often the case that we envision an end state: What will it look like when I have done this? However, we do not live in a Star Trek movie where we can simply beam ourselves from where we are to where we want to be. We need to engage in the journey that we need to take. Change always involves a degree of letting go of the past and engaging in a different future. Being unable to hold this transition (with all its emotional impacts) with insight and compassion can become a barrier to change.

William Bridges, in his 1991 book Managing Transitions: Making the Most of Change, looked at the psychological impact of change. He considered that change, as an external event such as a move, a new way of working, or reorganisation, is different from transition, which is the internal psychological process people go through to adapt. Bridges' model consists of three phases:

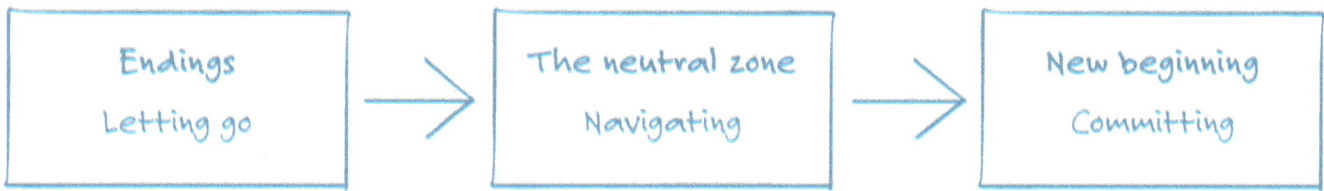

In reality, these phases overlap and run alongside each other, but like any journey, navigating the mid-journey (the neutral zone) is key. During this time, it may feel emotionally like you are living out of a backpack. You may feel uncertain of your path, you may feel lonely, and you may need to rely on some form of 'tourist information' and seek support from others.

> **SYNERGY: I feel this exists in my company the Mindfulness Association Poland – the four of us who have the task of the day-to day running of the organisation, as well as teaching courses. I feel there is a common goal of providing the best quality courses and retreats, and supporting each other in our personal and professional growth. Additionally, I feel that we also have strong connections with our international mentors and spiritual friends who continue to inspire and support us.**
>
> Anna Zubrzycki, *Sharing Your Treasure course participant*

Reflection Exercise: Journey Support

Take a moment now to sit and reflect on how you feel about the journey that you are embarking on and how that manifests itself for you.

- How can your practice support you to navigate the neutral zone?

- Who can support you on this journey, and how might connecting with your audience help you?

Reflection

Journalling Activity

There are two parts to this section's journalling, which you should write up here:

- Reflect on examples of serendipity/synergy that impact your plans for innovation.

- Think about what you might include in a 3-minute talk about your work/innovation. What would the bullet points look like?

Section 4

Altruistic Action

> **Changes came about because of a new point of view, essentially a new way of "being". Given the new point of view, all the actions changed naturally, smoothly, and all at once, not piece by piece. Extraordinary changes come from a new point of view – a new way of being. In this, as in all aspects of the game, 'being' precedes 'doing.**

Fred Shoemaker

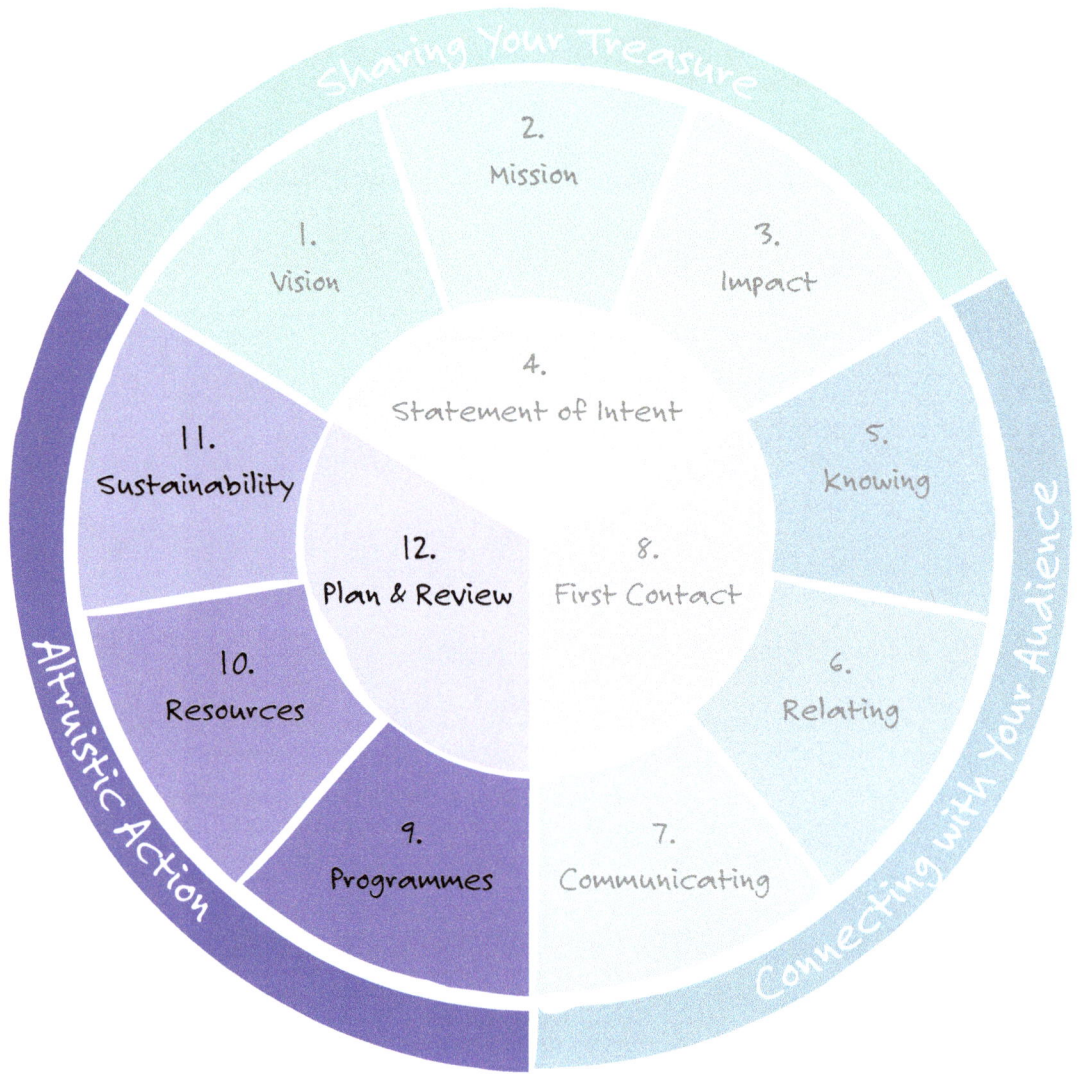

In this section, we will be exploring programmes, resources, and sustainability. Throughout this *Sharing Your Treasure* workbook, we have taken an inside-out approach to innovation, and we have looked at how this meets your passion to share your treasure as well as how it can help you to better connect with your audience. By the end of this section, you should be in a position to consider your business model.

In the previous section, you learnt to connect with the audience you intend to serve. Now it is time to design the programmes you want to offer and decide how much teaching you aim to do. What resources will you need to have in place to carry out your plan of action?

Even though you may not be motivated by how much money you will make from teaching mindfulness, it is important to have a financial reality check. A good question to ask yourself would be: What can I do to make my teaching financially sustainable so that I can continue doing the work I love?

When you review the twelve Fields of the Innovation Mandala, it will be apparent that the Fields are interconnected. There may be synergy or indeed conflicts between some of your priorities; enterprise is an art as well as a science. Can you find a way to engage in Altruistic Action that feels like a true reflection of your heartfelt aspirations to serve others?

❝ **Surprised:** I never thought this would be the way I would head when I signed up to this course. But now it also seems obvious, and I feel confident that I could deliver a good course that will have a positive impact on the lives of (hopefully!) lots of people. It aligns with my overall mission to wake up and help others to wake up.

Concerns: Will this be financially viable (especially the intro course)? I'll have to be careful to make sure this is sustainable (i.e. I get paid for the time I spend on it; I need to earn a living, and I can't offer it for free or next to nothing). I'm scared of spending a whole lot of time on it, and then it turns out I can't earn enough to cover my time. I can't sacrifice earning money elsewhere for this. This is my biggest concern.

Potential: If this is truly valuable, people will be willing to pay for it, and with the sliding scale, hopefully, those who can will be able to support others coming in. Also, I will need to explore ways to make it scalable. Plus, I have a habit of procrastinating because I think things will take a long time (sometimes they do!), but often the answer is right there and waiting. So my fears of how long it will take to design the course and get a pilot going might be unjustified. It might be much easier than I think, especially if I apply progress over perfection!

One step at a time, and only one way to find out – is to do it!

Jan Haworth, *Sharing Your Treasure course participant*

Reflection Exercise: Perceptions and Plans

Take a moment now to sit and reflect on your journey so far using this workbook. What have you become aware of, and how has this changed your perceptions and plans? How has this inside-out approach helped to prepare you to develop your business model?

Reflection

A Business Model

The concept of developing a business model can feel daunting, and an internet search of 'successful' examples can be intimidating rather than encouraging. It might help to view it as a 'project model', and it certainly doesn't have to be polished and highly formal. It may be helpful to call to mind the words of Bob Dylan…

"What looks large from a distance, close up ain't never that big".

In reality, writing your project model is probably akin to planning a group trip to the seaside – something that might sound big at first, but becomes manageable once you break it down: who's going, where you're headed, how you'll get there, and what everyone needs to bring. Like any good plan, the process is naturally broken down into common-sense steps.

The work that you have done throughout this workbook has led you to a point where you can start to bring it all together. Your project plan – whether you are planning to generate income or not from your ventures – brings together:

- Who you are
- Who you are called to serve
- Problem(s) you will solve

You should consider how busy you want to be. If you can quantify this and organise your plan around this, it will feel less daunting.

A Menu of Services

It is helpful to put together a menu, your programme, of what you are offering – presenting your services as clearly defined products. It is easier for an audience to relate to products and benefits than to services and features. This can provide a coherent sense of who you are, showing how different offerings fit together and are connected. Try to do this from your intended audience's perspective.

Keeping your plan and programme clear and simple helps it to become a personal compass as you move forward – outlining where you want (and do not want) to go. It also provides a clear message that can communicate to your audience what you stand for, if it is what they need, and whether they have come to the right place. It becomes a natural and authentic form of marketing.

Resources

As you develop your plan, you will need to consider what tangible and intangible resources you will need.

Some of the resources you need may be easily apparent, such as when and where you are going to run courses, access to IT, course materials, how much you need to charge, etc. Remember that your 'treasure' and your time are your biggest resources. Consider also the support and supervision that you will need.

Collaboration

An important resource to consider is who you might collaborate with. Collaborating with people that you want to work with can boost momentum and provide additional skills, insight and motivation. Collaboration can be a real game-changer and an opportunity for synergy.

Keep your Saw Sharp

It is important to remember your own personal wellbeing and professional development. This relates to the 7th Habit of Highly Effective People – sharpening your saw.

...but I don't have time to sharpen my saw – I need to cut this tree down!

Prioritising your work without carving out dedicated time for your physical, mental, social, emotional, and spiritual needs may lead to burnout – like trying to cut down a tree with a blunt saw. Taking the time to incorporate sharpening your saw into your plan will help your work to be sustainable.

Sustainability

So far, we haven't addressed the need for a financial model for your work. Taking an inside-out approach to innovation takes finance away from being a driving force behind sharing your treasure.

You may find it helpful to read Section 2.6 of the Fieldbook about business models at this stage.

Ask yourself how your financial model is aligned with who you are and who you serve. You will need to consider where the money is coming from and how much is actually needed. You may find that you are able to work collaboratively to generate income. Perhaps an employer or an organisation might support your costs or time?

Take some time to think creatively about your options.

Journalling Activity

Summarise your business model and create your 'menu' of services. After doing this take a moment to imagine yourself actually engaged in the activities to deliver, or work with others to deliver, these services. Does it feel right? If not, how might you change the plan?

Section 5

Plan & Review

❝ **I believe the time has come for the mindfulness community to stand up. Let us show the world that mindfulness can make a difference, a crucial difference; let us add its potential to what is already happening, out of compassion for future generations.**

Bhikkhu Anālayo

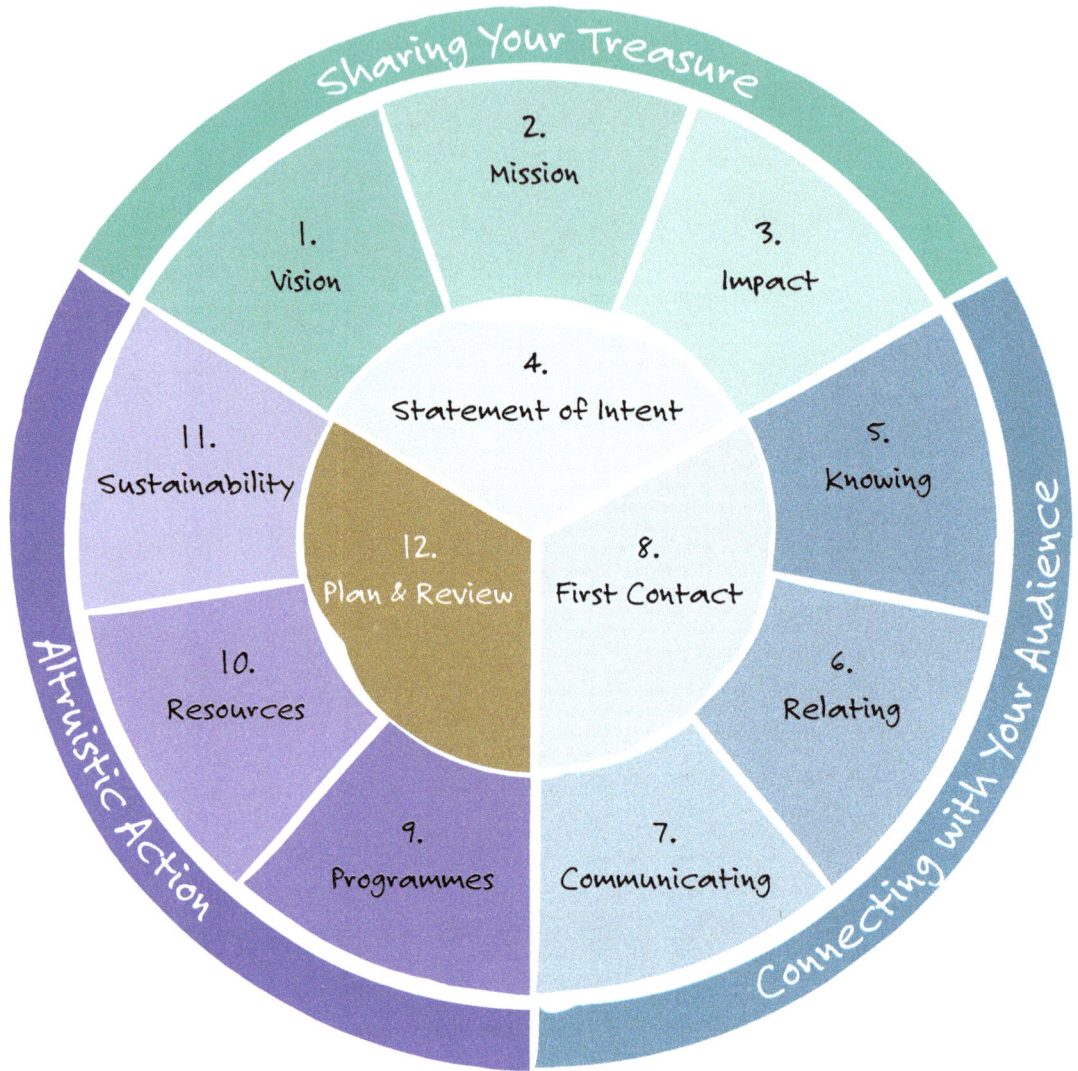

Developing Sharing Your Treasure: A Case Study in Itself

Taking some time here to walk through the process that we went through in creating this resource provides its own case study of the use of the Innovation Mandala.

Reflecting on two inspiring rounds of the Innovations in Mindfulness Awards, we posed the question – what more could we do to support and encourage the next wave of innovators, those at the very beginning of their journey or perhaps those who had reached a crossroads?

The next step was clear: to create an Innovations in Mindfulness Workbook as a companion to the Fieldbook. A resource that would make the core ideas more experiential, more personal, and more accessible. If the Fieldbook provides the principles of mindful innovation, the Workbook should offer a path for putting them into practice.

We began testing the approach through training, mentoring, and informal support for mindfulness teachers exploring new ways to innovate. A central outcome of this work was the Mindfulness Innovation Mandala – a framework that brings together key insights from innovation and enterprise, reimagined in a way that feels authentic and aligned with the perspective of mindfulness practitioners.

The Mandala was not intended as a linear process or a set of instructions. It is not a route map, but a reflective guide to deep personal exploration. It encourages teachers not to shape themselves into who they think they're supposed to be, but to ask a more courageous and fruitful question:

Not so much "What do I want to get?" but rather *"What do I have to offer?"*

We believe that this shift often leads to unexpected insights. The Mandala has been created to help teachers reflect on their own journey, identify the specific treasure they have to share, clarify the audience they feel called to serve, and design a sustainable structure to support their altruistic activity.

Innovation begins by asking, "What can I do now to make a difference?" and taking that first small step, which often opens new doors.

In 2025, we brought together our experience and insights into a new online course: Sharing Your Treasure. Based on the Innovation Mandala, the course invited mindfulness teachers to connect with their purpose and direction, and to support each other in bringing new ideas to life.

One of the most powerful elements of the course was the community that emerged. Participants from diverse backgrounds, with varied goals and challenges, came together to listen, encourage, and grow. Many shared a sense of relief when they no longer tried to fit into a mould but remembered to trust their personal experience and follow what felt most alive and authentic.

It became clear that innovation in mindfulness is a necessary evolution, a way of reconnecting with the deepest motivation that brought us to this work in the first place.

Growing out of this course and the work leading up to it, this *Workbook for Mindfulness Innovators* brings the Innovation Mandala to life. It is intended as a practical, interactive resource, a companion and guide, a feeling of community in book form. Its core features include:

- Explanations of each field of the Innovation Mandala
- Reflections and exercises to support readers on their own innovation journey
- Mini case studies, 'voices' from members of the innovation community, highlighting challenges, insights, and real-life turning points

The result of our work has been this workbook, produced especially for mindfulness teachers – both new and experienced – who are struggling to find opportunities in traditional formats, or who recognise it's time to do things differently. It's also for those who sense they have something unique to offer but don't yet know how to begin.

When teachers discover their unique niche, they not only serve others more effectively, but they also look after themselves more sustainably. These two goals are not in conflict; they are interdependent.

We hope that you can use the Mandala in the process that we have gone through to bring you this workbook.

Plan & Review: Key Learnings

Business Model – Project Design

A business model doesn't always need to be overly complex. Often, the simplest structure is the most effective, especially if it aligns with your personal vision and dream. The real value lies in crafting a strategy that feels authentic to you, rather than trying to mimic someone else's path. If the design fits your values, your lifestyle, and your ambitions, then it's "good enough" to start – refinement can come later as you grow.

Fail Fast – Fail Forward

Testing ideas quickly and affordably is one of the best ways to learn what works. By creating small experiments or prototypes, you minimise risk while maximising learning. This principle encourages action over endless planning. Every small test opens doors to unexpected opportunities and connections. Serendipity tends to find those who are already moving.

Two Circles

Think of two circles: one is your big dream (the long-term vision), and the other is your small start (what you can do right now). Real change happens where the two meet. Dreaming big keeps you inspired, while starting small keeps you grounded and practical. Your responsibility is to hold both truths: the courage to envision transformation and the humility to begin with manageable steps.

Remember Your Why

In the pursuit of goals, it's easy to become entangled in processes, tools, or even metrics, mistaking the method for the meaning. Coming back to your "why" keeps you anchored in purpose. Your "why" acts as both a compass and fuel: it helps you make better decisions when things get messy and gives resilience when challenges arise.

- **If We Waited Until Our Dance Was Pure...**

Motivations and plans are rarely perfect. But waiting until your plans and intentions are flawless before you begin will only lead to paralysis. The important truth is that by acting, even with imperfect plans, you allow good to emerge and grow.

- **Notice the Obvious**

Opportunities are often closer and simpler than we assume. Like mindfulness, this principle invites you to slow down and pay attention to what is right in front of you. Instead of chasing distant, complicated solutions, notice what's "low-hanging fruit" in your environment – a connection, a resource, or a step that is already available. Progress is often nearer, easier, and more accessible than we think.

Reflection Exercise: Three Key Questions

Take a moment to reflect on the following three questions, sensing the ease and feelings that finding the answers gives:

- What do I want to do?
- How can I make it work?
- Who can I work with?

Reflection

> **Never doubt that a small group of thoughtful, committed citizens can change the world; indeed, it's the only thing that ever has.**
>
> Margaret Mead

Journalling Activity

Going back over your reflections, how has the Mandala helped you to approach these questions? Is there one aspect of the Mandala that stands out for you, either as an area that has helped you or an area that you feel you need to work on? If you could commit to just one thing from the Innovation Mandala, what would it be and why?

Taking Stock of Your Journey

The aim of this workbook has been to provide a companion to help you innovate within the mindfulness space. At the heart of this offering is the Innovation Mandala, a reflective framework designed to help you uncover your own treasure – the unique gifts, experiences, and perspectives you have to offer. We hope that by taking an inside-out approach to innovation and journalling your path, you will have reached a point where your plans feel more tangible, authentic, and achievable. You may find that you are now in a very different place from where you expected to be at the end of this workbook, or you might feel that the place you are in is a familiar one. There is no right place to be, other than where you are right now. The journey continues.

What's Next

You may find it helpful to periodically review your journal that you have put together throughout this workbook. You may feel that you would like to revisit sections of the Mandala that have given you a sense of purpose, or you may wish to go over areas that you felt were more uncertain and unfamiliar to you.

We hope that you have found the workbook a useful tool, and we would like to remind you that you are not alone. We aspire to help mindfulness teachers find new ways to share their treasure with a world that needs mindfulness now more than ever. We encourage you to join our Innovations in Mindfulness Community to gain experience from others and continue to develop your ability to share your treasure and ensure its integrity.

Join our community and please stay in touch via:
www.innovationsinmindfulness.org/

Aditional notes

www.ingramcontent.com/pod-product-compliance
Lightning Source LLC
Chambersburg PA
CBHW061409070526
44584CB00032B/4200